Ole & Lena
LIVE via satellite

Featuring Bruce Danielson and Ann Berg as Ole and Lena

Photographer: Peter Roehrich

Book Design: Jonathan Norberg

Adventure Publications, Inc.
Cambridge, MN

DEDICATIONS

Bruce Danielson: I'd like to begin my dedication by thanking God for the many blessings he has given me and my family. Secondly, I dedicate this book to my parents, Vern and Jane, for instilling in me a love of humor. Next, to my sisters, Sandra and Peggy Jo, and my mother-in-law, Ruby, for their love and encouragement. Especially, I dedicate this book to my son, Matthew, for sharing in the joy of laughter and playing Little Ole so wonderfully for over ten years. But most of all, I dedicate this book to my wife Judy, the love of my life, who makes me laugh daily. She is my reason for living.

Ann Berg: To Larry, Justin, Ben and Adam, with laughter and love.

Ole and Lena: We dedicate this book to all of the people who have worked with us over the years in the annual variety show, having a ball while earning over $60,000 for scholarships for "our kids." We dedicate it to Dwight Maikkula (the originator of the show), Lynn Wedlund and the East Central Grad Band, John and Judy Lundeen, Dorcie Larson, the Abrahamson Sisters (Mary Falk, Delores Oslund, Joyce Swanson, and Darlene Fixell), Frank Wells as Einar Peterson, Becky Lieser and all her Georges (especially Bill Kruschel), Linda Pearson, Nancy Johnson, the Northwinds, Laurie Anderson, Lila Renstrom, Bob Theis, Bob Dolezal, Jack Hamargren and Fran McGivern as coordinators and avid supporters, the many members of our Ole and Lena Fan Club and the administrators, faculty members, and student volunteers that make the show happen every year in order to further the vocation of teaching.

Ole: Boy, Lena, ve owe a lot to a lot of people!

Lena: You can say dat again, Ole!

Ole: Boy, Lena, ve owe a lot to a lot of people!

ACKNOWLEDGEMENTS

Thanks to the following students, friends and colleagues who appeared in the book: Page 8: Matthew Danielson (Age 13); Page 10: Katina Eklund, Matthew Danielson (Age 22), Laura Ammon, Jennith Tarmann; Page 12 & 14: Adam Berg (Age 13); Page 24: (Guests) Jan Ludwigs, Barb Solomonson, Fran McGivern, (Bride & Groom) Eric Skow, Tanya Siedlecki; Page 32: Steven McIlllhargey; Page 34: Ray Petrie; Page 44: Marty Book; Page 50: Bailey Berg; Page 54: Norm Ayen; Page 56: (L to R) Stephanie Boesche, Gina Grant, Kelly Nutt; Page 62: Julie Sinner, Sally Johnson; Page 66: Patricia Peterson; Page 78: Bob Theis; Pages 80 & 82: Police Chief Rick Wilson; Page 84: Richard Capps.

Thanks to the following businesses and friends who lent supplies or locations and made this book possible: Cambridge American Legion Club, Cambridge Lutheran Church, Cambridge Mall, Central Rivers Agronomy Division of Isanti, Vernon Christensen, Domino's Pizza, Dr. Ed Hill, Gordie and Connie Hillstad, Herman's Bakery of Cambridge, Independent School District #911, Marcus Theatres, Patricia and Gary Peterson, Pet Supply Warehouse of Cambridge, Scott Sholund and the CIHS Girl's Swim Team, and the U.S. Post Office.

A special thank you to Peter Roehrich for his creative, photographic and technical skills that added so much to the aesthetic quality of the photographs and the imaginative quality of the book. Your input was invaluable.

Lena: Ole, da publisher says ve need a forevord to dis book.

Ole: A vhat?

Lena: A forevord.

Ole: Lena, knowing us, shouldn't it be a backvard?

Lena: How vould people read it?

Ole: Hold it up to a mirror, Lena. Do I haf to explain everyting?

FOREWORD

Ole and Lena jokes have been around since the first immigrants arrived in Minnesota over a hundred years ago; the real-life Ole and Lena have been around since 1989. That's when emcees of the local school and community variety show, Bruce Danielson and Ann Berg, were looking for some quick comedy acts to round out the program.

Ole and Lena skits were created to help accommodate scene and costume changes between numbers. But before long, it was obvious they were not content with a few bit parts! Audiences couldn't seem to get enough of the Scandinavian duo, so their roles were increased year after year. (Or, as Ole says, "Yah, Lena's rolls yust get bigger every year. So, ve yust get her bigger costumes!") At the present time, Ole and Lena actually run the show, now called the Kaleidoscope Revue, which has earned over $60,000 to award in scholarships in the past 14 years. They also perform at area potluck dinners and other events where lime jello actually is served! When Bruce and Ann aren't busy working as Ole and Lena, they teach in the Cambridge-Isanti school district in Minnesota.

TABLE OF CONTENTS

Meet the Olsons

(The Scandinavian Brady Bunch)

Lena wonders if Ole could ever love a girl like her.
Ole thinks he could, if she wasn't too much like her.

THE DAY OLE MET LENA

(Lena bats her eyelashes & flirts with Ole. He ignores her.)

Lena: (yells off) Officer, dis man is annoying me!

Ole: I never even spoke to you!

Lena: Yah, and dat is annoying me. I'm Lena. You are?

Ole: I'm Ole.

Lena: Hi, Ole. Do you haf a steady girlfriend?

Ole: No, I yust harvest da corn.

Lena: Oh, you play da field? I had a boyfriend, but ve disagreed on someting. I liked me and he didn't.

Ole: (shyly) I can understand dat.

Lena: (sits next to Ole) Yust da udder day, I vas looking in da pasture and I saw da cow and da bull rubbing noses. Kinda made me vant to do da same.

Ole: Go ahead, it's your cow!

Lena: Does dis remind you of anyting? (she puckers up)

Ole: Yah, Mama told me to bring home a toilet plunger!

Lena: Ole, you are playing hard to get, but by da time you get off da bus, you vill be crazy about me!

Ole: I'd haf to be crazy!

Ole never knew what true happiness was until he met Lena, and by then, it was too late!

THE DAY OLE PROPOSED

(Lena sits on a stool, shelling peas; Ole walks up nervously.)

Ole: It's a beautiful day, isn't it, Lena?

Lena: Anyting you say, Ole!

Ole: I haf a question to ask you, if it's OK vith you?

Lena: Anyting you say, Ole! But get down on vun knee to say it.

Ole: (as he kneels) Down on vun knee? Vy, Lena?

Lena: And ask it reeeel slow, Ole, so I can enjoy it.

Ole: OK, Lena. Mayyy I uuuuse yourrrrr ouuuthouuuse?

Lena: (disgusted) Anyting you SAY, Ole!

Ole: (as he walks away) Oh, and you vanna get married?

Lena: Ole, come back here and say dat again! Kneel, yah, kneel and say dat again reeeel sloooow.

Ole: (kneeling again) Mayyyy I uuuuuse yourrrr–

Lena: Not dat! Da udder ting about marriage!

Ole: Oh, dat! You vanna get married?

Lena: Anyting you say, Ole!!

[Ole claims that's the last time Lena's ever said those four words]

Ole and Lena named their last child when they heard about the world population on the radio. It said, "Every sixth child born in this world is Chinese."

OLE AND LENA'S CHILDREN

Ole: I am 100% Norvegian and Lena is 100% Norvegian; five out of six of our children are 100% Norvegian. It vas a sad day vhen da doctor broke da news dat our last child vould not be Norvegian. He said, "Ole, I'm sorry but dis child has to be born Caesarean."

Lena: But I tink dat's still Scandinavian, so dat's OK!

Ole: A couple of our children didn't look so good vhen dey vere born. Ve vere tinking of sending dem back and keeping da stork! In fact, da doctor took vun look at Little Ole and slapped Lena!

Lena: For da longest time, ve vondered vy Ole Junior's hair vas vhite. Den ve realized ve vas putting da talcum powder on da wrong end.

(I remember vhen Ole Jr. was born)

Doctor: Ole, you are the father of a baby boy!

Ole: Doc, does he look like me?

Doctor: When you hold him a certain way he looks like you, Ole, but you can't hold him that way long or the blood rushes to his head.

Ole: "I'd like you to meet Little Ole.
Some people say dere's a resemblance!"

OLE AND LITTLE OLE—EARLY YEARS

Ole: Little Ole is very smart. Some people say he got his brains from me. Vhat do you tink, Little Ole, did you get your brains from me?

Little Ole: I must haf, Papa. Mama still has hers!

Little Ole: Papa, I asked mama for help vith my homevork.

Ole: I told you never to go to Lena for help vith your homevork! Vhat stupid ting did she tell you to do?

Little Ole: To come to you!

Little Ole: Papa, vould you help me write a research paper on Eskimos?

Ole: Yah, you betcha. Vhat do you know about Eskimos?

Little Ole: Vell, ve eat dere pies!

Little Ole: Papa, I'm studying space travel. It seems dat everybody alvays vants to travel to da moon. I vant to be da first to travel to da sun!

Ole: Aren't you vorried about burning up?

Little Ole: Shows vhat you know, Papa. I'm going at night!

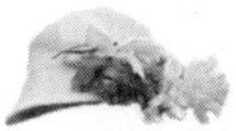

"Vanna Peck?"

"Vhat da heck?"

"Pain in da neck!"

OLE AND LITTLE OLE—COLLEGE YEARS

Ole: Now dat you're getting older, Little Ole, ve should haf a talk about dating.

Little Ole: Mama told me about your first date, Papa. She said she had to slap your face five times.

Ole: I vas getting fresh?

Little Ole: No, she tought you vere dead!

Little Ole: Papa, can I haf da car tonight? I've got a heavy date.

Ole: In dat case, take da truck!

Ole: You'd better be good vhen you're datin' dese girls, Little Ole. Do you know dat I never even kissed your mama until after ve vere married? Now, vill you be able to say da same ting to your children?

Little Ole: Yah, Papa, but not vith as straight a face as you yust did.

Little Ole: Classes are going vell in college, Papa. In science, I'm proving a theory dat diarrhea is hereditary, 'cuz I found some in my genes!

Littler Ole may be warm, but the can of paint said "Requires two coats."

LENA AND LITTLER OLE

Lena: So, Littler Ole, how did you like going to school today?

Littler Ole: Oh, I liked going, and I liked coming home. It's dat in-between part I could do vithout.

Lena: Vhat did you study today in school, Littler Ole?

Littler Ole: Ve studied da stars and da universe. Da teacher told us dat a comet vas a star vith a tail.

Lena: Could you name vun?

Littler Ole: Yah, Lassie.

Littler Ole: Our math teacher tought she could stump us vith a hard question. She asked, "Dis may take you a vhile to figure, but how many seconds are dere in a year?"

Lena: Dat must haf taken a lot of figuring, Little Ole.

Littler Ole: No, I hardly had to tink. I told her twelve.

Lena: Twelve?

Littler Ole: Yah, January 2nd, February 2nd, March 2nd...

Littler Ole wonders why he should give the fish more water.
They didn't drink what he gave them yesterday.

LENA AND LITTLER OLE 2

Littler Ole: Mama, I tink I made my teacher mad today.

Lena: Vy should today be any different? Vhat did you do?

Littler Ole: He vas trying to confuse me vith a question. He said, "Littler Ole, if three men dig three holes in three days and it takes seven days to take a round trip to da moon, den how old am I?" I said, "Dat vould make you 60 years old." He said, "Dat's right! How did you know?" I said, "'Cuz my aunt is 30 and she's only half nuts!"

Lena: Let's prepare for da science quiz, Littler Ole, vhat is da shape of da vorld?

Littler Ole: Lousy!

Lena: No, its shape! Like da shape of my earrings.

Littler Ole: Square.

Lena: No, da vuns I vear on Sundays.

Littler Ole: Round.

Lena: So now, vhat is da shape of da vorld?

Littler Ole: Square on veekdays and round on Sundays.

OLE'S FAVORITE STORIES: 4TH RUNNER-UP

Ole and the Cuckoo Clock

Ole's side of the story:

Vun night, I stayed out late playing cards vith da boys. As I valked in da door, da cuckoo clock vas striking 3 o'clock in da morning. So Lena vouldn't know I came in dat late, I yust cuckooed 8 more times and Lena believes I came in at 11. She's so easy to fool!

Lena's side of the story:

Ole and I need to get da cuckoo clock fixed. Da udder night, at 11 o'clock, it cuckooed 3 times, gave off a "shh!" sound, hiccupped 4 times, burped twice, yelled "Uffda!," den cuckooed 8 more times. *(So I tink it's time somevun cleaned Ole's clock!)*

Distant Relatives

(but not distant enough!)

Ole carries this picture of his mother-in-law, may she rest in peace–soon!

OLE'S MOTHER-IN-LAW

Ole: I've tried to get along vith my mudder-in-law. Vhen Lena and I vere first married, I told her, "Mudder Svenson, our house is your house," so she sold it!

Ole: Lena's mudder doesn't haf ulcers, but she's a carrier!

Ole: She used to valk right into our house (vithout even knocking) and slam da door behind her. Vun time, she slammed it so hard, da cuckoo clock above da door came smashing down to da floor. If it had fallen three seconds sooner, it vould haf killed her. Dat clock has alvays been slow!

Ole: She has a bad habit of complaining, like vhen she complains, "Ole, dis old apartment is soooo hot." I say, "Get used to it. Dat's vhat eternity's going to be like for you!" (She laughs; she tinks I'm kiddin'!)

READERS: Can you spot my mudder-in-law in da picture? She's da vun dat's sitting down and holding baby Lena. You've heard da expression: Her face vould stop a clock? Vell, her face vould stop Svitzerland!

Ingeborg is leaving her body to science,
but science is contesting the will.

LENA'S SISTER, INGEBORG

Lena: Ole, my sister is soooo beautiful!

Ole: Lena, she is so wrinkled dat vhen she vears long earrings, she looks like a venetian blind.

Lena: Ole, my sister vas alvays so popular! She could haf married anyvun she pleased.

Ole: Too bad she never pleased anyvun!

Lena: Ole, don't forget dat ve're going to Ingeborg's dis veekend for her 39th birthday party.

Ole: Lena, ve vent to Ingeborg's 39th birthday party ten years ago. In fact, I remember da 39 candles on da cake, and dat vas yust on da piece I vas eating.

Lena: Vait 'til you see my sister; she's had a facelift.

Ole: She tried dat before, Lena, but it did no good. Dey lifted her face and da vun underneath vas yust as ugly as da first vun! Plus, if she has dat face lifted vun more time, she's going to haf to close da top of her blouse to hide her belly button.

Historical Trivia: While talking to Ingeborg in 1975, Ole was inspired to invent the first cordless phone.

LENA'S SISTER, INGEBORG 2

Ole: Lena, I yust got off da phone vith Ingeborg.

Lena: Vhat did she vant, Ole?

Ole: Oh, da usual. She complained how I acted at her vedding all dose years ago. She felt dat if I vanted to throw rice at her, I should haf taken it out of da 50-pound bag first.

Lena: Talk nice about her; she's got da face of a saint.

Ole: Yah, a Saint Bernard!

Lena: Ole, men swarm around her.

Ole: No, Lena, flies swarm around her!

Ole: Ingeborg is so ugly dat vhen she sent her picture to an ugly contest, dey wrote back, "Sorry, no professionals!"

Ole: Vhen Ingeborg vas born, da doctor looked at both ends and said, "Oh, Siamese Tvins!" She couldn't play in da sandbox, 'cuz da cat kept covering her up! She vent to a plastic surgeon; he vanted to add a tail!

Ole'a first clue that Ingeborg's husband wasn't too bright was when he needed help finding his way out of church.

INGEBORG'S HUSBAND

Ole: I von't say dat Ingeborg's husband is stupid, but if his IQ vas four points higher, he could be a plant.

Ole: Lena, Ingeborg's husband had a terrible accident da udder day. He vas horseback riding and his foot got caught in da stirrup of da saddle. Da horse bucked him off and he could haf been killed!

Lena: Vhat happened den, Ole?

Ole: Tank goodness for da quick-tinking store manager. He ran over and unplugged da darn ting.

Lena: Ole, you need to quit accusing Ingeborg of henpecking her husband. Like most husbands, he alvays gets da last vords in.

Ole: Yah, Lena, and dose vords are, "Yes, dear!"

Lena: Vhen Ingeborg and her husband fight, she alvays comes crawling back to him on her hands and knees.

Ole: True, Lena, she is on her hands and knees. But vhat she's saying is, "Come out from under dat bed and fight like a man!"

A recent sighting at the Immigration Office.
(Who says history doesn't repeat itself?)

RELATIVES FROM THE OLD COUNTRY

Lena: Ole, remember my uncle dat came over from Norvay and became rich using yust three little vords?

Ole: Vhat three little vords?

Lena: "Stick 'em up!"

Ole: Den, Lena, dere vas my uncle who got drafted by da Norvegian Army at da age of 40.

Lena: Vy so old?

Ole: 'Cuz da Army vanted dem fresh out of high school.

Ole: Ingeborg's husband brags dat his ancestors came over on da Mayflower. Dat's lucky for dem, Lena, 'cuz da immigration laws are so much stricter now!

Ole: Remember dat gold-digger, Lena, dat only married your uncle 'cuz his father left him $100,000?

Lena: Dat's not true, Ole. She vould haf married him no matter who had left him $100,000.

Ole: Ve knew your uncle vasn't bright vhen he came into dis country. On da application, it said "Sign Here" and he put "Aquarius!"

OLE'S FAVORITE STORIES: 3RD RUNNER-UP

Ole Loves Ice Fishing

Ole thought he should take up ice fishing so he had something fun to do in the winter. His first experience with it was not too good. As he sat on the ice wondering why he wasn't catching anything, he heard a voice from up above. "Ole, you must get off the ice!" He was shocked, of course. "Vy, Lord? Is dere going to be a storm and you're trying to save me? Is dere trouble at home and you're varning me to get dere soon? Are you trying to help me by showing me vhere da fish are biting? Tell me, Lord, vy haf you come to me?" The reply came, "Ole, this is the Zamboni driver! You must get off the ice!"

Jobs

Statistics show that the average American will change careers seven times during their life.

(Ole changes seven times in one month!)

Ole's latest job: a male striper!

OLE'S JOBS

Ole: I lost my yob again, Lena, but it vasn't my fault dis time. Da boss told me to do vhatever da signs say.

Lena: So, vhat did da sign say?

Ole: "Vet Floor."

Ole: Lena, I got dat yob dat I vanted vith da circus!

Lena: Ole, I'm so excited for you!

Ole: Sorry, Lena, dey fired me. I vas supposed to be da man dey shot out of da cannon, but dey vanted a man of higher caliber.

Lena: Ole, how is da yob going vith da highvay department?

Ole: I got fired, Lena! I vas supposed to be painting da yellow lines down da highvay. Da first day, I painted over three miles, da next day three blocks, and da third day, only three feet. So, dey fired me.

Lena: Ole, vy did you get so slow?

Ole: Lena, every day it vas so much further to valk back to da paint can!

"Who threw up on da lefse?"

(Ole's job at the pizza house lasted 12 minutes.)

OLE'S JOBS 2

Lena: Ole, vhat happened to your new yob vith da telephone company?

Ole: I don't know, Lena. I vas supposed to be putting telephone poles in da ground but dey fired me 'cuz in a veek's time, I only got vun put in.

Lena: Vun? I saw da udder vorkers. Dey vere getting four or five a day!

Ole: Yah, but did you see how much of dere poles stuck out of da ground?

Ole: Vell, Lena, I got fired again!

Lena: Ole, you only lasted two days at da cuckoo clock repair shop. Vhat happened?

Ole: Vell, dey claim dat after I repair a cuckoo clock, da bird backs out of da door, turns around, scratches his head, and asks vhat time it is.

Ole: Lena, I got a new yob as a pilot!

Lena: Ole, how can you be a pilot?

Ole: Easy, Lena, I got a yob at da stable. I pile it over here, I pile it over dere...

This customer's mistake was to say he was in a hurry, so get him a cup of coffee, a doughnut and step on it!

OLE AND LENA'S FIRST JOB

Ole and Lena's first job was in a restaurant. Its buffet said: "ALL YOU CAN KEEP DOWN FOR $3.92." They were the waiter and waitress.

Lady: (Impatiently) Waiter, will my pancakes be long?

Ole: No, dey'll be round, as usual.

Man: Waiter, I see a piece of wood in my cottage cheese.

Ole: Vhat vere you expecting for 50¢, da whole cottage?

As Lena waitresses, she overhears some men talking romantically to their wives. One man says, "Pass the sugar, Sugar." Lena thinks, "Vhat a lover!" Another man looks at his wife and says, "Pass the honey, Honey!" Again, Lena thinks, "Vhat a lover!" So she decides to see if Ole can't be that romantic too.

Lena: Say someting like dat to me, Ole.

Ole: Pass da tea, bag!

Lena: Ole, I saw dat husband nibble on his vife's ear and kiss her again and again. Vy can't you do dat?

Ole: I hardly know da voman, Lena!

Ole on his way to the White House

OLE'S WHITE HOUSE DREAMS

Ole: I yust got off da phone vith Ingeborg. She says dat dere is no vay she vould vote for me for President. In fact, she says she vouldn't vote for me if I vere St. Peter himself. I told her dat if I vas St. Peter, she vouldn't be in my district.

Ole: Vun of my first actions as President vould be to pass a law dat makes it possible to make gasoline out of manure. It may not make great gasoline, but it vill sure cut down on da siphoning problem.

Ole: Ingeborg got mad at Lena recently and told her dat ve vere da perfect couple for politics."Who better," she said, "to symbolize da donkey and da elephant den Ole and you?"

Ole: I tink it vould be best to keep our distance from your sister and her family during da election, Lena.

Lena: Vy, Ole? Vhat's wrong vith Ingeborg's family? She has a son in college vith a 4.0 average.

Ole: Lena, dat's not his grade point average, dat's his blood-alcohol level! He hopes to graduate Magna cum Loaded!

"I haf alvays told da truth,
but if elected, I promise to change!"

OLE'S PRESS CONFERENCE

Ole: Who vould like to ask me da first question?

Newsman: Is it true the IRS has asked for your records?

Ole: Yah, dey did. And I took dem two of my Lawrence Velk, three Mitch Miller, and a Tijuana Brass.

Newswoman: Mr. Olson, if your family has any skeletons in the closet, it would be best to tell us now.

Ole: Vell, my brudder is in trouble because he alvays does vhat he is told. Da udder day, his vife told him to drop his pants at da cleaners. His case comes up next Vednesday. Den, dere is my aunt who's very superstitious. She vunce believed dat because she broke a mirror, she vould haf seven years of bad luck.

Newswoman: Did she have seven years of bad luck?

Ole: No, she died da next day!

Newsman: Mr. Olson, presidents often bring their pets to the White House. I hear you will be bringing your pet zebra. What is his name?

Ole: Ve named him Spot.

OLE'S FAVORITE STORIES: 2ND RUNNER-UP

Ole Gets a Job as a Rich Man's Butler

Ole worked for a very rich man who had a beloved Persian cat. When the man went on a business trip, he left the cat in Ole's care. A week later he phoned home.

Man: How are things, Ole?

Ole: Fine...yust fine.

Man: And how is my beloved Persian cat?

Ole: Oh, she's dead.

Man: How dare you tell me so bluntly about my beloved Persian cat?!

Ole: But she vas dead! Vhat should I haf said?

Man: Well, you could have broken it to me gently...when I called, you could have said, "She's up on the roof and we can't get her down!" The second time, you could have said, "She fell off the roof but is recuperating nicely." And the third time, you could have said "She died peacefully in her sleep."

Ole: I'm sorry. It vill never happen again.

So the man resumed his trip and called home a week later.

Man: How are things, Ole?

Ole: Fine...yust fine.

Man: And how is my beloved Mother?

Ole: Oh, she's up on da roof and ve can't get her down.

Hobbies

Ole has plans for his spare time,
if Lena ever gives him any!

Ole has told Lena before never to name the worms.
It makes it so hard to use them as bait.

OLE LOVES FISHING

Lena: Ole, I vill never believe you again! First, you told me ve vere going on a cruise, and ve end up in dis lousy fishing boat! Den, you told me it vould be soooo romantic, it vould take my breath avay.

Ole: Doesn't it take your breath avay, Lena?

Lena: Yah, but only 'cuz I'm doing all da rowing!

Lena: Ole, vy can't Ingeborg ever come fishing vith us?

Ole: Because, Lena, she eats all da bait!

Ole and his good friend, Einar Peterson, went fishing one Saturday. Einar showed Ole the new thermos he found at the hardware store. "It keeps hot tings hot and cold tings cold," Einar boasted. "So, vhat haf you got in dere, Einar?" Ole asked. Einar replied, "Coffee and popsicles."

Einar: I'm glad ve took up fishing. Ve veren't very good at moose hunting; da decoys vere too heavy.

Ole: Ve veren't very good at duck hunting, neither, Einar. Maybe ve veren't throwing da dogs up high enough.

Ole wants to go fishing! Are you game, Warden?

OLE AND THE GAME WARDEN

Game Warden: Evening, sir! How ya doin'?

Ole: I am doing great, tanks for asking!

Game Warden: Had much luck today?

Ole: Luck? I haf never been luckier!

Game Warden: Really? How so?

Ole: Vell, I caught about twelve valleyes.

Game Warden: Did you say twelve walleyes?

Ole: Uh-huh! And about fifteen bass and twenty muskies.

Game Warden: Oh? Do you know who I am?

Ole: No, who are you?

Game Warden: I'm the Game Warden.

Ole: Uh-oh. Ummm.... Do you know who I am?

Game Warden: No, who?

Ole: Da biggest liar in da state of Minnesota!

Ole claims Lena will buy anything marked "down."
He says that yesterday, she tried to buy an escalator.

LENA AND SHOPPING

Ole: Lena, look at da shirt you bought. It's only half dere. Don't tell me it's because it vas marked 'Half Off.'

Lena: Ole, don't be silly! I bought it for your half brudder.

Lena was shopping for a new outfit for herself. She found a very expensive sweater made of virgin wool. When Ole saw the price, he suggested she look for something a little cheaper, maybe something from a sheep that fooled around a little bit.

Lena: Ole, you yust need somevun to shop for. Vy don't you buy a birthday gift for my sister, Ingeborg.

Ole: Lena, I vouldn't know vhat to buy for Ingeborg.

Lena: Ole, buy her someting dat goes vith her looks.

Ole: Like vhat? Horseshoes?

When Ole, Jr. was born, Lena was shopping for a really good price on cloth diapers. The clerk rang up her purchase and said, "That'll be ten dollars, plus tax!" Lena replied, "Oh, ve don't plan to use tacks. Ve plan to use safety pins."

Lena wonders why the computer keeps saying she's got mail. Ole was able to find the mouse, but doesn't know where to plug it in.

OLE AND LENA AND TECHNOLOGY

(WARNING: If you are allergic to puns, avoid this page)

Lena: Ya know da best part about computers, Ole? It's da vunderful cow boxes.

Ole: Dose cow boxes are *udderly* fantastic, Lena.

Lena: You'll get no *beef* from me about dat, Ole.

Ole: No matter how *cheesy* da computer is, da box is yust vunderful.

Lena: Dis computer is *butter* den our neighbor's, Ole.

Ole: Vhat do you tink, Lena? Haf ve *milked* dis enough for now?

You can always tell when Ole has been using the new computer; there's "white-out" on the screen.

Lena: Ole, I vas yust getting used to da new computer. Vy are you making us pack it up and send it back?

Ole: Rules are rules, Lena.

Lena: Vhat rules, Ole?

Ole: Lena, da varranty said "Return vithin seven days of purchasing." Ve can't argue vith da varranty!

Ole and Lena have finally found a member of their family that likes Lena's cooking.

LENA'S COOKING

Lena: I make two dishes really vell. Vun is Svedish Meatballs and da udder is lime yello!

Ole: (looking at his plate) Vhich vun is dis, Lena?

Ole: Lena, you are da only woman I know dat takes an hour to cook minute rice. Who else do you know who has to ask somevun how to boil vater? And vhile ve're at it, how many people need to look up da recipe for ice cubes?

Lena: Are you finished yet?

Ole: Vhen I see a sign dat advertises "Home Cooking," I right avay get heartburn.

Lena: (in tears) Ole! After all da sacrifices I make to put dinner on da table...

Ole: Sacrifices? I don't call 'em sacrifices, I call 'em burnt offerings!

Lena: Ole, I vant a new dress. Yust look at me! If anyvun came to da door and saw me in dis dress, dey'd tink I vas da cook.

Ole: Dey'd change dere mind if dey stayed for supper!

Why isn't fishing ever on Lena's To-Do-List?

HOME IMPROVEMENT

Lena: Ole, I haf a whole list of tings for you to do dis summer. Da first vun on da list is to move da house six inches to da north.

Ole: Lena, vy vould ve move da house six inches north?

Lena: To take up da slack on da clothes line.

Lena: Ole, remember how you carpeted da bathroom last summer?

Ole: Yah, Lena, you loved da new carpeting in da bathroom.

Lena: So, dis summer, let's carpet all da vey up to da house.

Einar: (holding a nail with the point toward him) Tanks, Ole, for picking up da nails, but you got da kind vith da heads on da wrong end.

Ole: Don't be silly, Einar. Dose are for da udder side of da house.

Ole: Lena, you're alvays anxious to get rid of unvanted tings, so vhen da nursing home called asking for donations, I gave dem your parents!

Judge: Are you a pole-vaulter?

Ole: No, I'm Norvegian, and don't call me Valter!

OLE AND THE OLYMPICS

Lena: Ole, pleeze enter a safer event dis Olympics.

Ole: Vhat vas wrong vith last time, Lena?

Lena: Ole, who's ever heard of a javelin catcher?

Ole: But, you must admit, I did pretty vell in it, Lena.

Lena: Vell, it's easy vhen you're da only vun who lived.

Lena: Ole, didn't you haf an uncle in da Olympics?

Ole: Yah, Lena, but he vasn't too bright.

Lena: How could you tell?

Ole: He von a gold medal and had it bronzed!

Lena: Ole, if you ask me, your best event vould be da svimming event. Remember dat time you dove into dat pool of sharks at da zoo and svam da length of it in record time?

Ole: Yah, Lena, and I'm still lookin' for da smart aleck dat pushed me in.

The Olympic Committee may use Ole as a torch. It might be his only chance to be bright!

Lena claims they all cheated on the breaststroke!
She's sure they used their arms!

LENA AND CONTESTS

Lena: Dey should haf an event at da Olympics for da best lookin'.

Ole: Lena, dat's a beauty contest, not da Olympics. And how vould dat do you any good? You entered dat beauty contest at da County Fair and your three brudders vere da judges. Who von dat time?

Lena: My father! But dat doesn't mean I couldn't vin somevhere else.

Ole: Dat's true. You entered da Mrs. America Contest dat time and I tink you only missed vinning dat contest by two feet.

Lena: Two feet?

Ole: Yah, twelve inches on vun hip and twelve inches on da udder hip.

Lena: Ole, you need to put someting on dat black eye vhen ve get home.

Ole: I don't haf a black eye, Lena.

Lena: Ve aren't home yet, neither!

Ole: Lena did vin a contest vun time. She vas visiting da Swine Barn, leaned in to look at vun more closely, and dey pinned a blue ribbon on her.

OLE'S FAVORITE STORIES: 1ST RUNNER-UP

Ole and the Magic Lamp

Vhen Lena and I vere valking on da beach vun day, I came across a magic lamp. I did vhat Lena says I alvays do, I rubbed it da wrong vay, and guess vhat came out? A genie! He said he vould grant me my biggest vish. To be unselfish, I showed him a map of da Middle East and asked for peace in dat area of da vorld. I told him I vanted dis group of people to get along vith dat group of people. He explained dat my vish vas vay too big for him, so pleeze vish for someting more reasonable and he'd grant me dat vun for sure. So I tought and I tought. I said, "Genie, I vant all Norvegians to be rich, good lookin' and smart!" He said, "Show me dat map again!"

Up Close & Personal with Ole & Lena

Things you've always wanted to know, but didn't care enough to ask!

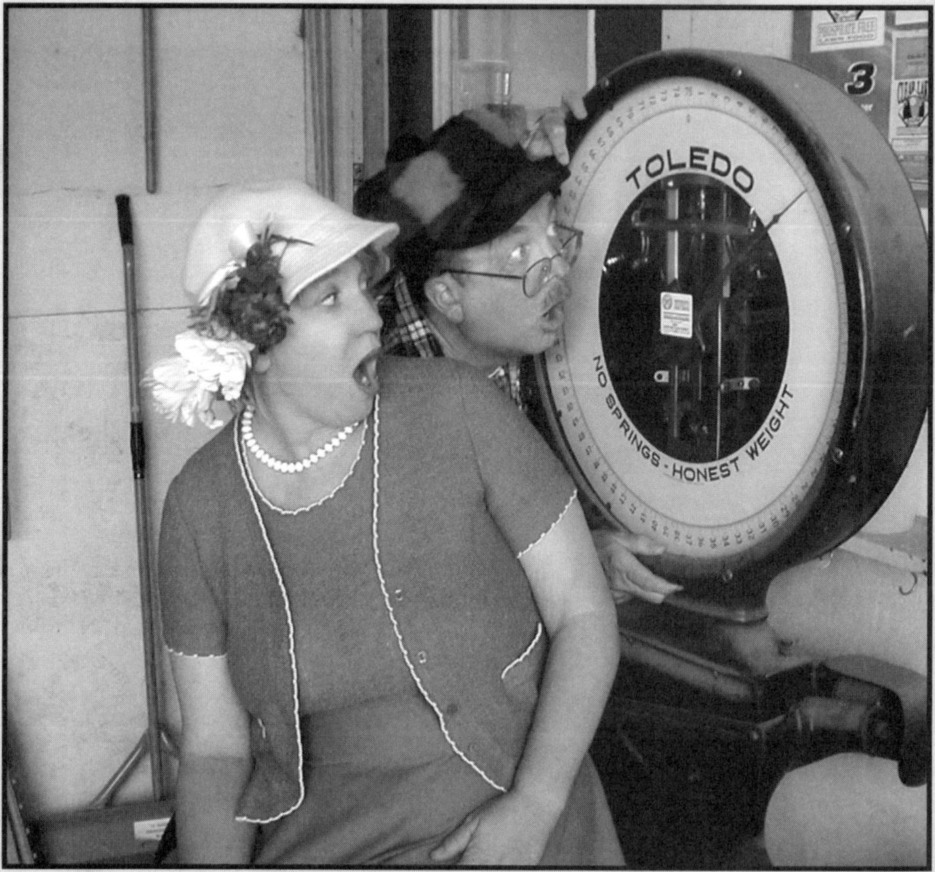

It's not that Lena's big, but she's got an unlisted dress size!

LENA'S WEIGHT

Ole: Lena, how do you like our new scale?

Lena: I don't! I never vanted a scale dat talked.

Ole: Vy, Lena, vhat did it say to you?

Lena: Last time I stepped on it, it said, "Vun at a time, pleeze!"

Doctor: Ole, when did Lena first know she had a weight problem?

Ole: Vhen her senior picture had to be taken by an aerial view. It appeared on pages 52, 53 and 54.

Doctor: Have things gotten any better?

Ole: I don't tink so. Now da bathtub has stretch marks!

Lena: Ole, vhen I vent to see da doctor, he told me I had da perfect body.

Ole: Vait a minute, Lena. Da doctor told you dat you had da perfect body? Vhat did he say about your big rear end?

Lena: Funny, he never mentioned you!

Ole told Lena never to wear blue
when standing near a mailbox.

LENA'S WEIGHT 2

Ole: I von't say dat Lena is heavy, but vhen her beeper goes off, people tink she's backing up! Lena's shadow alone veighs twelve pounds. I shouldn't tease Lena about her veight. She's da only ting I've ever invested in dat's doubled in size. Lena is big! It's not everyvun whose underpants haf mud flaps! Lena's measurements? Vy, dey're 58-36-45. But not necessarily in dat order!

Lena got hit while in a pedestrian crossing. She asked the driver why he didn't just drive around her. He said, "I didn't think I had enough gas!"

Ole: Lena, how is da new rowing machine vorking out?

Lena: Not too good, Ole. Last night, I vas rowing on it and it sunk!

Lena recently sang in church. One of the parishoners commented to Ole that Lena had a large repertoire. Ole answered, "It's yust her dress dat makes it look dat big!"

Since Lena's not really moving, Ole wishes she'd quit asking, "Are ve dere yet?"

EXERCISING

Ole: Lena, I see dat you are trying to exercise and lose some veight.

Lena: Yah, Ole. Last veek I tried horseback riding and I took off ten pounds.

Ole: Off you or off da horse?

Lena: Ole, I finally figured out how to get rid of 180 pounds of ugly fat: yust get rid of you!

Lena: Ole, now dat I've gotten to know your brudders and your sisters, I must say your mudder must haf been very strong!

Ole: How vould she haf gotten so strong, Lena?

Lena: From constantly raising dumbbells!

Ole: Lena, how is dat new aerobics class going for you?

Lena: Oh, I qvit dat, Ole. Every veek vas da same story: I'd push and I'd pull, I'd grunt and I'd stretch, I'd viggle and I'd squirm, and by da time I had da leotards on, da class vas over!

The teacher would like to speak to the head of the household, but she'll have to settle for Ole.

A CALL FROM SCHOOL

Teacher: May I speak to Mr. Olson?

Ole: Yah, dat's me.

Teacher: Mr. Olson, your son is having trouble in school.

Ole: Now vait yust a minute. Vhen I haf trouble vith him in da summer, do I call you?

Teacher: (under her breath) Now I see where he gets it.

Teacher: Mr. Olson, he doesn't seem to be listening. The other day, after studying American History, I asked him how the Liberty Bell got cracked and he wasn't able to tell me.

Ole: Vell, he's pretty honest. If he says he didn't crack it, den I vould tend to believe him.

Teacher: (long pause) May I speak to Mrs. Olson?

Ole: No use, she didn't crack it neither.

Ole: Ya know, Miss Thomlin, raising kids is not easy, especially teenagers. Lena and I look back to da time vhen ve used to rock dese kids in da cradle, and somedays, ve vished ve'd used bigger rocks!

This experience brings back old memories for Ole.
Déjà vu all over again!

A CALL FROM SCHOOL 2

Teacher: Mr. Olson, your son is constantly late to school. He blames it on walking his bike to school.

Ole: He valks it? Vy doesn't he ride it?

Teacher: That's what I asked him. He said that he is so late already, he doesn't have time to get on it.

Ole: Oh? Vell, as long as he has a logical reason.

Teacher: Due to his behavior, I am afraid we are going to have to remove your son from the school play.

Ole: I didn't know about da play. Vhat part did he haf?

Teacher: He played an older man who's been married for 25 years.

Ole: Vell, maybe next time he'll get a speaking role.

Teacher: Well, I must go. I was glad to see you at conferences. I hope to see more of you!

Ole: More of me? Dis is all dere is of me!

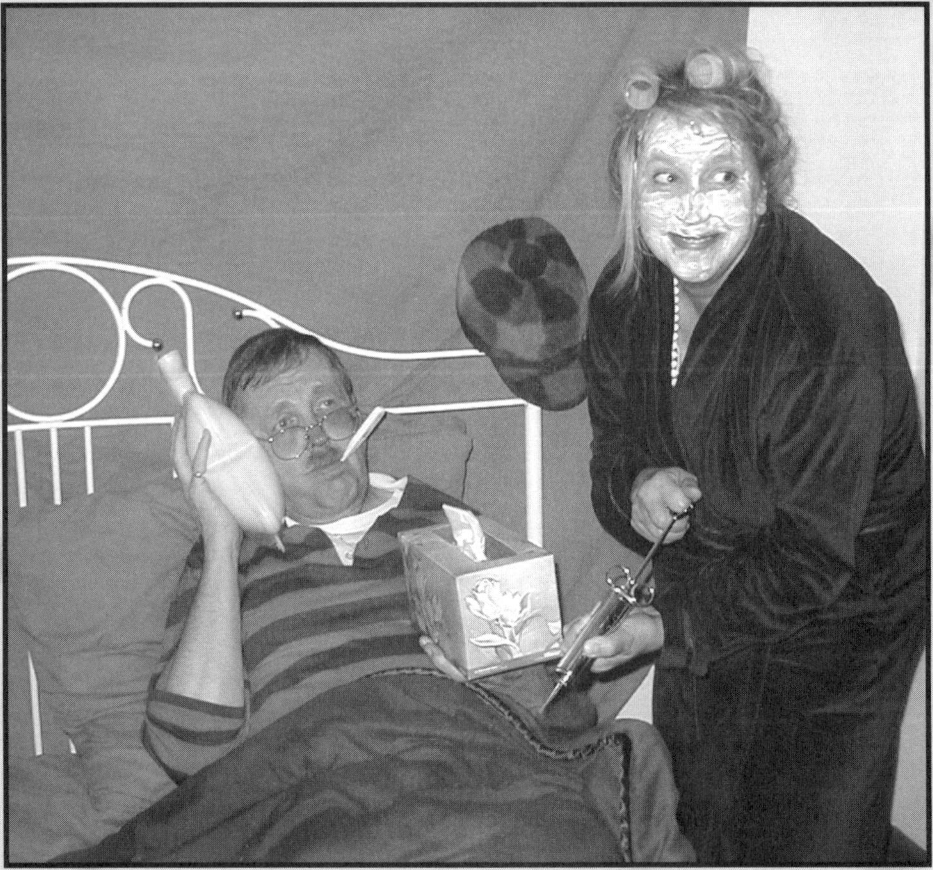

Ole: Lena, vith friends like you, who needs enemas?

OLE'S ILL / NEAR DEATH

Ole: (calling from bed) Lena, dat hotdish sure smells good. Can I haf some for supper?

Lena: Ole, you know I'm saving dat for da funeral!

Lena has already given thought to Ole's obituary. Since there is a price break for five words or less, she's planning to print: "Ole's dead / Boat for Sale."

Ole: I'm vorried dat vhen I die, Lena may be so happy, she vants to dance on my grave. So, if dat's her plan, I'll show her! I'll be buried at sea!

Lena: (complaining) Da voman across da road has had three husbands. All of dem haf died and she's had all three cremated! Da reason I'm upset? I had trouble getting vun husband and she's got husbands to burn!

READERS: You'll be happy to know that Ole has fully recovered from this illness. He had $6,000 in medical bills and it was just flatulence.

(That goes to show the high price of gas these days!)

OLE'S FAVORITE STORIES: THE #1 WINNER

Ole and the Hotel Clerk

The Olsons stayed at a hotel that advertised "One full week for $100," but at checkout:

Clerk: That will be $175 please.

Ole: $175? Vhere did da udder $75 come from?

Clerk: Well, there are certain extras that we add on. $25, for example, for use of the sauna.

Ole: Ve never used da sauna!

Clerk: No, but it was there if you'd wanted to. And $25 for use of the swimming pool.

Ole: Ve never swam in da pool.

Clerk: No, but it was there if you'd wanted to. And $25 for use of the 18-hole golf course.

Ole: Golf course? Vy, ve never–

Clerk: No, but it was there if you'd wanted to.

Ole gave him $100 and when he asked why:

Ole: I'm charging you $75 for kissing Lena!

Clerk: I never kissed your wife!

Ole: No, but she vas dere if you'd vanted to!

Vacation

Come travel with Ole & Lena–it's a real trip!

Ole: I tink da problem might be da kitchen sink!

OLE AND LENA'S VACATION

Part I: Loading the car

Lena: Vill you get in da car, Ole? I vant to get going on our vacation to Mount Rushmore.

Ole: No, Lena, I von't get in until you promise me ve are really going to Mount Rushmore. Every year you promise ve are going somevhere, but ve alvays end up in Minot, Nort Dakota, visiting your sister, Ingeborg.

Lena: Get in, Ole. Ve are going to Mount Rushmore!

Ole: (getting in) Good!

Lena: By vay of Minot, Nort Dakota.

Ole: Lena!

Lena: Ole, remember last year vhen ve vent to Disneyland?

Ole: Yah, I remember. You said ve vere going to Disneyland, but ve ended up in Minot. Now, I know Minot is a Mickey Mouse town and your brudder-in-law is goofy, but dat doesn't make it Disneyland!

Lena: Yust relax, Ole, let's make dis a great vacation!

Ole: OK, let's go see Mount Rushmore and da five stone faces.

Lena: Mount Rushmore only has four stone faces, Ole.

Ole: Yah, but ve're also going to see your sister!

Lena: Ole, are ve dere yet?

Ole: Lena, ve yust pulled out of da driveway!

OLE AND LENA'S VACATION

Part II: The Trip

Lena: So, Ole, ve're on our vey!

Ole: Vhat haf you got in dat bag you're carrying, Lena?

Lena: I've got some apples, Ole. Tell you vhat; if you can guess how many I've got, I'll give you da both of 'em.

Ole: I guess three.

Lena: Nope, missed it by two.

Ole: Did you bring da newspaper, Lena?

Lena: No, I wrapped da garbage in it, Ole.

Ole: Oh, Lena, I vanted to see it!

Lena: Vell, it vas yust some orange peels and some old coffee grounds!

Ole: Remind me dat vhen ve get to Minot, I haf to do vhat da doctor told me for my backache. He told me dat I haf to take a bath in milk.

Lena: Vy a bath in milk, Ole?

Ole: 'Cuz da cows are too short for me to take a shower.

Lena: Must da milk be pasteurized?

Ole: No, Lena, yust up to my chin!

Attendant: Should I check the dipstick?

Ole: No tanks, Lena's doing yust fine.

OLE AND LENA'S VACATION

Part III: Hours Later—Stopping For Gas

Lena: Ole, vhile you get some gas, I'll check out da map.

Ole: OK, Lena.

Attendant: Good morning, sir!

Lena: (distracted, looking at map) Vhat did he say?

Ole: (to Lena) He said, "Good morning." (to Attendant) Good morning.

Attendant: What'll you have: regular or unleaded?

Lena: (distracted) Vhat did he say?

Ole: (to Lena) He asked if ve vanted regular or unleaded. (to Attendant) Unleaded, please.

Attendant: Beautiful day! Where are you headed?

Lena: (distracted) Vhat did he say?

Ole: (to Lena) He asked vhere ve're headed. (to attendant) Ve're going to Minot, Nort Dakota.

Attendant: I was in Minot once, and walking down the street, I saw the ugliest woman I've ever seen!

Lena: (distracted) Vhat did he say?

Ole: (to Lena) He says he knows your sister!

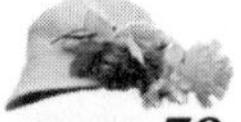

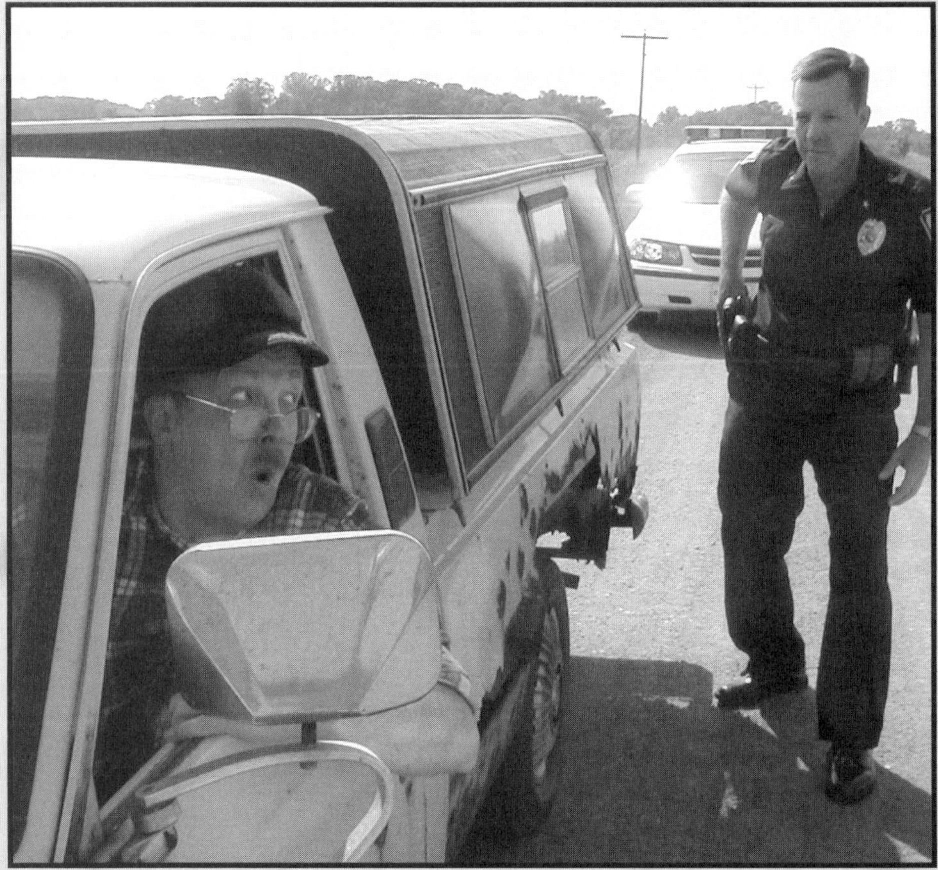

Ole: Here comes da police! Play dumb!

OLE AND LENA'S VACATION

Part IV: Hours Later—Stopped & Copped

Lena: Ole, dere's a car vith a red light going round and round behind us.

Ole: Yah, Lena, he must vant to get around us and catch some criminal, so I'll yust pull over.

Lena: Ole, he stopped too. He's coming up to da car.

Ole: Lena, vhatever you do, don't show him your driver's license!

Lena: Vy, Ole?

Ole: I don't vant him to see dat you got an F in sex.

Policeman: (leaning in driver's window) Yup, 65, at least!

Lena: No, it's yust dis hat dat makes me look dat old.

Policeman: No, ma'am, I mean your husband was travelling over the speed limit. Doing 65, at least.

Ole: I vas not!

Policeman: You were too!

Ole: I vas going 45!

Policeman: You were not!

Ole: Your radar is wrong!

Policeman: It is not!

Lena: Officer, officer, it's no use arguing vith Ole vhen he's been drinking.

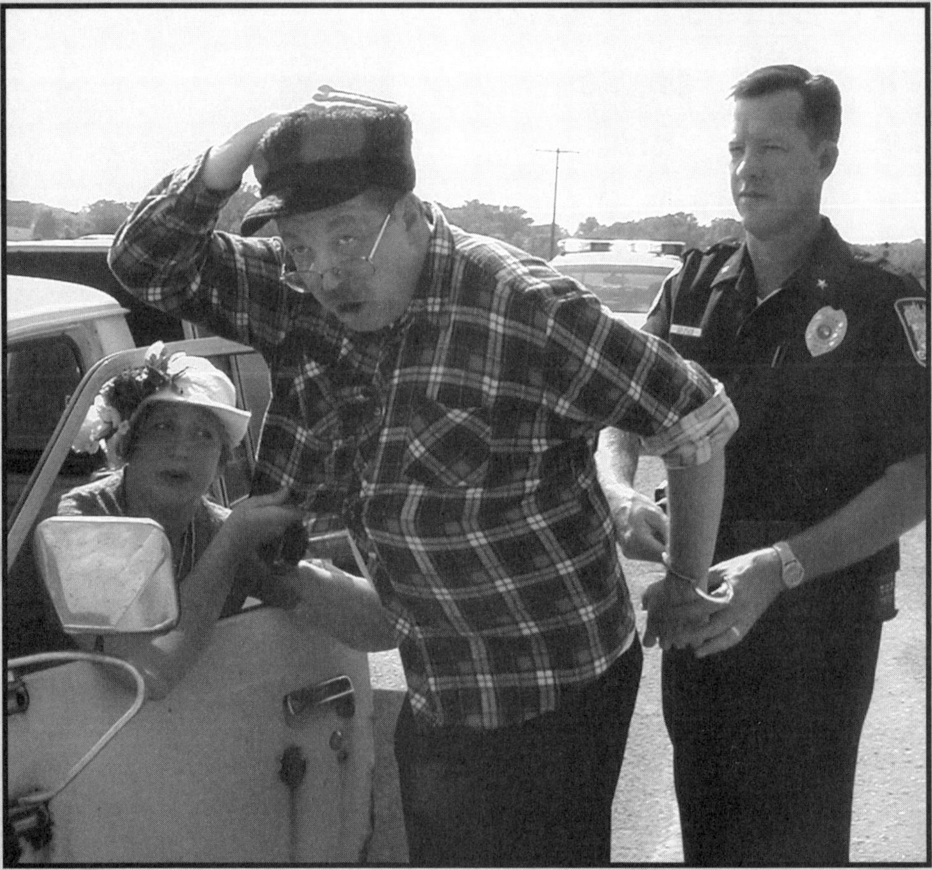

Ole: You can't take me avay! Vhat about da people reading dis book?

Policeman: Who do you think sent me to get you?

OLE AND LENA'S VACATION

Part V: Ole Gets booked

Ole: Lena, vhat are you saying? Who's side are you on?

Lena: Dis is no time to choose sides, Ole. Yust go quietly vith da nice policeman.

Ole: (to Policeman) Vhat are you going to do vith me?

Policeman: I'm going to book you.

Ole: But, but, speaking of books, vhat about dis book? If you take me avay, how vill ve complete dis book?

Policeman: I wouldn't worry about that, it's on its last pages anyway.

Ole: Vhat about da sequel? Ve plan to call it "*Ole and Lena Live Via Satellite: Doing #2*."

Policeman: Then consider this a huge favor to the readers!

Here was the Fan Club the first year. Since they had limited members, Richard Capps became the President, Vice President, Treasurer and Secretary.

FAN CLUB APPLICATION

Ole: If you've enjoyed da humor in dis book and vould like to receeve more of it, pleeze join da Ole and Lena Fan Club. You vill receeve qvarterly newsletters (three times a year), a signed Ole and Lena picture, and two surprises from da club during da year.

Lena: All of da money raised by da Fan Club membership fee is given to scholarships for students going to school to become teachers. So how can you lose?

OLE AND LENA FAN CLUB APPLICATION

DUES: $10 per year ($1 per month)

Name:____________________son **Nickname**:______________ **Born:** Yes/No

Age: Under 39/39/Over 39 **Nationality:** Norvegian/Udder **Hair Color:**_____

Eyes:_____ **Eye Color:** Right_____ Left_____

Circle: Married or ~~Happy~~ Single **Years of Marriage:** 0-5/5-10/10-20/Life

Unemployed from Vhat Job?____

Higher Education (over 3rd grade)____

Fan Club Benefits: An autographed picture of Ole & Lena, a quarterly Newsletter (three times a year), two fun surprise gifts during the year

Valk, don't run, and mail dis to:
Ole and Lena Fan Club, c/o CIHS, 430 NW 8th Ave., Cambridge, MN 55008

ALL FAN CLUB DUES GO TOWARD CIHS SCHOLARSHIPS!

Bruce's Biography:
This is a photo of Judy, Bruce and Matthew Danielson in October 2000, following a formation at which Bruce was promoted to Staff Sergeant Major in the Minnesota Army National Guard. Judy is an instructional Assistant at Isanti Elementary School in Isanti, Minnesota. Bruce has taught math, English and speech at Cambridge-Isanti High School in Cambridge, Minnesota for 17 years as well as being in the MNARNG for 29 years. Bruce previously taught math at St. Wenceslaus Catholic School in New Prague, Minnesota for 11 years. Their son, Matthew (22), who played Little Ole for ten years, graduates in May 2002 from the University of St. Thomas in St Paul with a degree in Math Education. Bruce and Judy have been married for 30 years and live in Cambridge, Minnesota with their Miniature Schnauzers Harry (3) and Sam (1).

Ann's Biography:
Ann is a graduate of the College of St. Benedict and St. Cloud State University, and teaches English, reading and special education. She also is an adjunct professor at Hamline University. Ann lives with husband Larry, sons Justin, Ben and Adam, and fur kids Noah and Bailey. She enjoys attending her sons' sporting events and relaxing at the cabin "up north."